KAFFIR
BOY

Mark Mathabane

WRITERS' VOICES

ATTENTION READERS: We would like to hear what
you think about our books. Please send your comments
or suggestions to:

Signal Hill Publications
P.O. Box 131
Syracuse, NY 13210-0131

• • •

SIGNAL HILL®

PUBLICATIONS

Selection: From KAFFIR BOY by Mark Mathabane.
Copyright © 1986 by Mark Mathabane.
Reprinted by permission of Macmillan Publishing Company.

Supplementary materials
© 1991
Signal Hill Publications
An imprint of New Readers Press
U.S. Publishing Division of Laubach Literacy International
Box 131, Syracuse, New York 13210-0131

10   9   8   7   6   5   4   3   2

First printing: March 1991

ISBN 1-929631-28-5

The words "Writers' Voices" are a trademark of
Signal Hill Publications.

Cover designed by Paul Davis Studio
Interior designed by Paolo Pepe

Acknowledgments

We gratefully acknowledge the generous support of the following foundations and corporations that made the publication of WRITERS' VOICES and NEW WRITERS' VOICES possible: An anonymous foundation; The Vincent Astor Foundation; Booth Ferris Foundation; Exxon Corporation; James Money Management, Inc.; Knight Foundation; Philip Morris Companies Inc.; Scripps Howard Foundation; The House of Seagram and H.W. Wilson Foundation.

This book could not have been realized without the kind and generous cooperation of the author, Mark Mathabane, and his publisher Macmillan Publishing Company. Thanks also to Judith Fernandez Latham.

Our thanks to Paul Davis Studio and Myrna Davis, Paul Davis, Jeanine Esposito, Alex Ginns and Frank Begrowicz for their inspired design of the covers of these books. Thanks also to Paolo Pepe for his sensitive design of the interior of this book, Karen Bernath for design of maps and diagrams, and to Ron Bel Bruno for his timely help.

CONTENTS

Note to the Reader

Kaffir Boy is a true story. It is the autobiography of Mark Mathabane. (His last name is pronounced MOTT-uh-bahn-eh.) In this book he tells what it was like to be a young black person growing up in South Africa in the 1960s and 1970s.

Every writer has a special voice. That is why we call our series *Writers' Voices*. We chose *Kaffir Boy* because it lets you hear the voice of Mark Mathabane—a black South African struggling to survive the cruel racism in his country. In choosing parts from the book, we wanted you to hear Mark Mathabane tell about how racism affected his life at a very young age and how he and thousands of other young people began to rebel against it in 1976.

Reading "About the Selections from *Kaffir Boy*" on page 10 will help you begin thinking about what you will read in the selections.

In addition to selections from *Kaffir Boy*, this book includes chapters with interesting and helpful information related to the selections. You may read these before or after reading the selections. You may choose to read some or all of these chapters.

• If you would like more information about South Africa and the history of the relationship between blacks and whites in that country, look at the chapter called "About South Africa" on page 55.

• If you would like more information about the system of apartheid—the laws of South Africa keeping blacks and whites apart—look at the chapter called "About Apartheid" on page 60.

• In the chapter "About Mark Mathabane" on page 52, you will find information that is not in the selections from his autobiography. Sometimes such information will give you more insight into the selections.

If you are a new reader, you may want to have this book read aloud to you, perhaps more than once. Even if you are a more experienced reader, you may enjoy hearing it read aloud before reading it silently to yourself.

We encourage you to read *actively*. Here are some things you can do.

BEFORE READING

- Read the front and back covers of the book, and look at the cover illustration. Ask yourself what you expect the book to be about.

- Think about why you want to read this book. Perhaps you have heard about South Africa and want to know more about that country.

- Look at the Contents page. See where you can find a map of South Africa, which shows the places mentioned in the book, and other information. Decide what you want to read and in what order.

DURING READING

- There may be special words that have to do with South Africa or other words that are difficult to read. Mark Mathabane sometimes uses the British spelling for words (like *neighbourhood*) rather than the American spelling (*neighborhood*). Keep reading to see if the meaning becomes clear. If it doesn't, go back and reread the difficult part or discuss it with others or look to see if it's in the glossary on page 44 or look up the word in the dictionary.

- Ask yourself questions as you read. For example: What would it be like to live in

South Africa if you were black? If you were white?

AFTER READING

● Think about what you have read. Did you identify with Mark Mathabane? Did you learn something new about South Africa? Did any of your ideas about South Africa change because of what you read?

● Talk with others about your thoughts.

● Try some of the questions and activities in "Questions for the Reader" on page 47. They are meant to help you discover more about what you have read and how it relates to you.

The editors of *Writers' Voices* hope you will write to us. We want to know your thoughts about our books.

About the Selections from *Kaffir Boy*

At the beginning of *Kaffir Boy*, Mark Mathabane tells why he wrote the book. This is what he says:

"I am always asked to explain what it felt like to grow up black under South Africa's system of legalized racism known as apartheid, and how I escaped from it and ended up in America. This book is the most thorough answer I have heretofore given.

The last thing I ever dreamed of when I was daily battling for survival and for an identity other than that of inferiority and fourth-class citizen, which apartheid foisted on me, was that someday I would attend an American college, edit its newspaper, graduate with honors, practise journalism and write a book.

How could I have dreamed of all this when I was born of illiterate parents who could not afford to pay my way through school, let alone pay the rent for our shack and put enough food on the table; when black people in Alexandra lived under constant police terror and the threat of deportation to impoverished tribal reserves; when at ten I contemplated suicide because I found the burden of living in a ghetto, poverty-stricken and without hope, too heavy to shoulder; when in 1976 I got deeply involved in the Soweto protests, in which hundreds of black students were killed by the police, and thousands fled the country to escape imprisonment and torture?

In *Kaffir Boy* I have re-created, as best as I can remember, all these experiences. I have sought to paint a portrait of my childhood and youth in Alexandra, a black ghetto of Johannesburg, where I was born and lived for eighteen years, with the hope that the rest of the world will finally understand why apartheid cannot be reformed: it has to be abolished.

Much has been written and spoken about the politics of apartheid: the forced removals of black communities from their ancestral lands, the Influx Control and Pass laws that mandate where blacks can live, work, raise families, be buried; the migrant labour system that forces black men to live away from their families eleven months out of a year; the breaking up of black families in the ghettos as the authorities seek to create a so-called white South Africa; the brutal suppression of the black majority as it agitates for equal rights. But what does it all mean in human terms?

When I was growing up in Alexandra it meant hate, bitterness, hunger, pain, terror, violence, fear, dashed hopes and dreams. Today it still means the same for millions of black children who are trapped in the ghettos of South Africa, in a lingering nightmare of a racial system that in many respects resembles Nazism. In the ghettos black children fight for survival from the moment they are born. They take to hating and fearing the police, soldiers and authorities as a baby takes to its mother's breast. . . ."

The selection from *Kaffir Boy* has two parts. The first part takes place in 1965, when Mark Mathabane was five years old.

His family lived then in a tiny shack in Alexandra, near Johannesburg. Johannesburg is South Africa's largest city. Alexandra was then a district of one square mile, with 100,000 blacks, mixed-race people and Asian Indians crammed into it.

Blacks were needed in cities such as Johannesburg to do the low-paying, menial jobs. But they were forbidden to live in these cities. Instead they were forced to live in poor, all-black areas like Alexandra.

The adults had to carry passbooks for identification. These passbooks, issued by the government, were meant to control the lives of non-whites in and near the cities. People caught without them were immediately arrested. (You'll find more information on the system of apartheid on page 60.) They were either sent to jail or sent out to the homelands. There, they lived in extreme poverty.

The police would make surprise visits to shantytowns such as Alexandra, looking for gangsters and for people who did not have passbooks or for black families living illegally in the township.

As Part One begins, Mark Mathabane's family is awakened in the middle of a cold winter night by the sounds of a police raid.

In the dark and cold, Mathabane's mother has to hide. She does not want to be rounded up by the police. They will check her passbook and say it is not in order. She has to leave five-year-old Mark in charge of his three-year-old sister Florah and his baby brother George.

Perhaps Part One will make you think about a time when you were young and very frightened.

*   *   *

Part Two of the selection takes place when Mathabane is 16. The white government–ruled Department of Bantu Education decided to force all black schools to teach their courses in Afrikaans instead of English. The blacks were angry that Afrikaans was being forced on them.

On June 16, 1976, a large group of students in Soweto decided to form a protest march. The peaceful student marchers were suddenly fired on by the police. Many were killed or wounded. The next day, Mark Mathabane and most of his classmates and teachers decided that they too would march peaceably to show their support of the Soweto students.

Mathabane tells about these protests and what happened next.

Perhaps Part Two of the selection will remind you of some decision you made that helped other people (or yourself) overcome injustice.

South Africa has undergone many changes since the events in *Kaffir Boy* took place. See the chapters "About South Africa" and "About Apartheid" to read further about changes in South Africa.

SELECTED FROM
KAFFIR BOY

Mark Mathabane

PART ONE

"Don't go, Mama!" I cried. "Please don't go! Don't leave us, please!"

She did not answer, but continued opening the door a little wider and inching her blanketed body, still bent low, slowly forward until she was halfway in and halfway out. Meantime in the bedroom George continued bawling. I hated it when he cried like that, for it heightened, and made more real, my feelings of confusion, terror and helplessness.

"Let him suck thumb," my mother said, now almost out of the house. She was still bent low. She spat on the doorknob twice, a ritual that, she once told me, protected the innocent and kept all evil spirits away, including the police. I felt vaguely reassured seeing her perform the ritual.

"And don't forget now," she said, "don't ever be afraid. I'll be back soon." Those were her last words; and as I watched her disappear behind the shacks, swallowed up by the ominous darkness and ominous sounds, her figure like that of a black-cloaked ghost, she seemed less of the mother I knew and loved, and more of a desperate fugitive fleeing off to her secret lair somewhere in the inky blackness.

I glanced at the window; it was getting light outside. I saw two black policemen breaking down a door at the far end of the yard. A half-naked, near-hysterical, jet-black woman was being led out of an outhouse by a fat laughing black policeman who, from time to time, prodded her private parts with a truncheon. The storm of noises had now subsided somewhat, but I could still hear doors and windows being smashed, and dogs barking and children screaming. I jerked George and pinned him against the window, hoping that he would somehow understand why I needed him to shut up; but that did not help, for his eyes were shut, and he continued to scream and writhe. My eyes roved frantically about the semidark room and came to rest on a heavy black blanket hanging limply from the side of the bed. Aha! I quickly grabbed it and pulled it over George's head to muffle his screams. I pinned it tightly with both hands over his small head as he lay writhing. It worked! For though he continued screaming, I could hardly hear him. He struggled and struggled and I pinned the blanket tighter and tighter. It never crossed my mind that my brother might suffocate. As he no longer screamed, I waited, from time to time glancing nervously at the window.

Suddenly I heard the bedroom door open and shut. Startled, I let go of my hold on the blanket and turned my head toward the door only to see Florah, her eyes wild with fear, come rushing in, screaming, her hands over her head. She came over to the bedside and began tugging frantically at the blanket.

"Where's Mama! I want Mama! Where's Mama!"

"Shut up!" I raged. "Go back to sleep before I hit you!"

She did not leave.

"I'm scared," she whimpered. "I want Mama."

"Shut up, you fool!" I screamed at her again. "The white man is outside, and he's going to get you and eat you!" I should not have said that; my sister became hysterical. She flung herself at the bed and tried to claw her way up. Enraged, I slapped her hard across the mouth; she staggered but did not fall. She promptly returned to the bedside and resumed her tugging of the blanket more determinedly. My brother too was now screaming. My head felt hot with confusion and desperation; I did not know what to do; I wished my mother were present; I wished the police were blotted off the surface of the earth.

I could still hear footsteps pounding, children screaming and dogs barking, so I quickly hauled my sister onto the bed, seeing that she was resolved not to return to the kitchen. We coiled together on the narrow bed, the three of us, but because of all the awkward movements everyone was making, the bricks propping the legs of the bed shifted, and it wobbled as if about to collapse. I held my breath, and the bed did not fall. I carefully pulled the blanket tautly over the three of us. Under the blanket I saw nothing but darkness.

But the din outside after a temporary lull surged and made its way through the bolted door, through the barricade, through the kitchen, through the blanket, through the blackness and into my finger-plugged ears, as if the bed were perched in the midst of all the pandemonium. My mind blazed with questions. What was really going on outside? Were the barking dogs police dogs? Who was shooting whom? Were the *Msomi** gangs involved? I had often been told that police dogs ate black people when given the order by white people—were they eating people this time? Suppose my mother had been apprehended, would the police dogs eat her up too? What was happening to my friends?

I ached with curiosity and fear. Should I go to the kitchen window and see what was going on in the streets? My sister had wet the bed, and it felt damp and cold. Childish curiosity finally overcame the fear, and I hopped out of bed and tiptoed to the kitchen window.

With mounting excitement I raised myself toward the window and reached for the flap. I carefully pushed it to one side as I had seen my father do and then poked my head through; all the time my eyes were on

*Legendary black gangsters of the fifties and early sixties in the mode of the Mafia.

the prowl for danger. My head was halfway in and halfway out when my eyes fell upon two tall black policemen emerging from a shack across the street. They joined two others standing alongside a white man by the entrance gate to one of the yards. The white man had a holstered gun slung low about his waist, as in the movies, and was pacing briskly about, shouting orders and pointing in all different directions. Further on in the yard, another white man, also with a gun, was supervising a group of about ten black policemen as they rounded up half-naked black men and women from the shacks. Children's screams issued from some of the shacks.

The sight had me spellbound. Suddenly the white man by the entrance gate pointed in the direction of our house. Two black policemen jumped and started across the street toward me. They were quickly joined by a third. I gasped with fear. A new terror gripped me and froze me by the window, my head still sticking halfway out. My mind went blank; I shut my eyes; my heart thumped somewhere in my throat. I overheard the three black policemen, as they came across the street, say to each other:

"That's number thirty-seven."

"Yes. But I don't think we'll find any of the *Msomi* gang in there."

"*Umlungu* [the white man] thinks there may be a few hiding in there. If we don't find them, we can still make easy money. The yard is a haven for people without passbooks."

"But I think everybody has fled. Look at those busted doors."

"There's a few over there still shut."

"All right, then, let's go in."

Suddenly there was a tremendous thud, as of something heavy crashing against the floor, and I heard George's screams of pain pierce the air. I opened my eyes momentarily and saw the three black policemen, only a few steps from the door, stop and look at one another. I quickly retracted my head but remained crouched under the window, afraid of going anywhere lest I be seen. I heard the three policemen say to one another:

"You heard that?"

"Yes. It's an infant crying."

"I bet you they left that one alone too."

Suddenly my sister came screaming out of the bedroom, her hands over her head.

"Yowee! Yowee!" she bawled. "Johannes! Come an' see! Come an' see!"

I stared at her, unable to move, not wanting to move.

"It's G-george," she stammered with horror, "b-blood, d-dead, b-blood, d-dead!" her voice trailed into sobs. She rushed over to where I stood and began pulling my hand, imploring me to go see my brother who, she said dramatically, was bleeding to death. My mouth contorted into frantic, inaudible "Go aways" and "Shut ups" but she did not leave. I heard someone pounding at the door. In the confusion that followed angry voices said:

"There's no point in going in. I've had enough of hollering infants."

"Me too."

"I bet you there's no one in there but the bloody children."

"You just took the words right out of my mouth."

"Then let's get back to the vans. We still have more streets to comb. This neighbourhood is about dry anyway."

They left. It turned out that George had accidentally fallen off the bed and smashed his head against a pile of bricks at the foot of the bed, sustaining a deep cut across the forehead. The gash swelled and bled badly, stopping only after I had swathed his forehead with pieces of rags. The three of us cowered together in silence another three hours until my mother returned from the ditch where she had been hiding.

PART TWO

No one thought it would happen, yet everyone knew it had to happen. All the hate, bitterness, frustration and anger that had crystallized into a powder keg in the minds of black students, waiting for a single igniting spark, found that spark when the Department of Bantu Education suddenly decreed that all black schools had to teach courses in Afrikaans instead of English.

The first spontaneous explosion took place in Soweto on the afternoon of Wednesday, June 16, 1976, where about ten thousand students marched through the dirt streets of Soweto protesting the Afrikaans decree. The immense crowd was orderly and peaceful, and included six- and seven-year-olds, chanting along with older students, who waved placards reading: To Hell with Afrikaans, We Don't Want to Learn the Language of Our Oppressors,

MAP OF PLACES MENTIONED
IN THE SELECTIONS

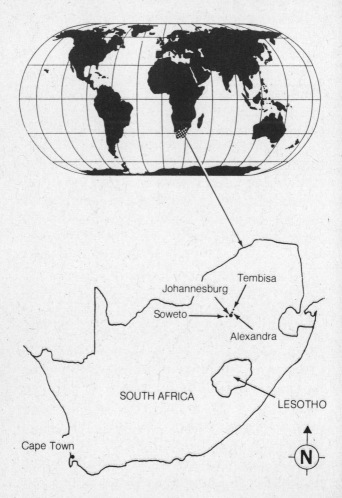

Stop Feeding Us a Poisonous Education and We Want Equal Education Not Slave Education.

Unknown to the marchers, along one of the streets leading to Phefeni High School, where a protest rally was to be held, hundreds of policemen, armed with tear gas canisters, rifles, shotguns and *sjamboks*, had formed a barricade across the street. When they reached the barricaded street the marchers stopped, but continued waving placards and chanting:

"AMANDLA! AWETHU! AMANDLA! AWETHU! (POWER IS OURS! POWER IS OURS!)"

While student leaders argued about what to do to defuse the situation, the police suddenly opened fire. Momentarily the crowd stood dazed, thinking that the bullets were plastic and had been fired into the air. But when several small children began dropping down like swatted flies, their white uniforms soaked in red blood, pandemonium broke out.

The police continued firing into the crowd. Students fled into houses alongside the street; others tripped, fell and were trampled underfoot. Some were so shocked they didn't know what to do except scream and cry. Still others fought bullets with rocks and schoolbags. One youth saw a thirteen-year-old go down, a bullet having shattered his forehead. He picked the dying boy up, and carried him to a yard nearby. The photo of the two—the lifeless boy in the hands of a youth whose face blazed with anger, hate and defiance—made headlines around the world.

In the school bus from Tembisa, reading the gruesome accounts of what took place in Soweto in the late afternoon edition of the *World*, I felt hate and anger well up inside me. I cried. The entire edition of the *World* was devoted to the story. One of the pictures of the carnage showed a hacked white policeman near an overturned, burnt police car, surrounded by groups of students shouting defiant slogans, fists upraised in the black power salute. I gloated, and wished that more white people had been killed.

The bus was packed, yet silent. Heads were buried inside newspapers. Tears flowed freely down the cheeks of youths returning from school, and men and women returning from work. I again looked at the photo of the two boys, and then and there I knew that my life would never, could never, be the same again.

"They opened fire," mumbled David, who was sitting alongside me, shaking his head with disbelief. "They didn't give any warning. They simply opened fire. Just like that. Just like that," he repeated. "And small children, small defenseless children, dropped down like swatted flies. This is murder, cold-blooded murder."

There was nothing I could say in reply, except stare back. No words could possibly express what I felt. No words could express the hatred I felt for the white race.

"This is the beginning of something too ugly to contemplate," David said. "Our lives can, and should, never be the same after this."

I nodded.

At school assembly the next day, the mood was somber. There was tension in the air. There was a fire, a determination, in students that I had never seen before. The first thing the principal said was, "I guess you've all heard about the tragedy that took place in Soweto yesterday."

"Yes," the crowd of students roared.

"It is indeed a dark moment in our lives,"

the principal said. "But we here have to go on learning. The government has ordered all other schools to stay open. I'm sure things will settle down and will return to normal soon."

A murmur of disapproval surged through the crowd. One student in the back row shouted, "There can be no school while our brothers and sisters are being murdered in Soweto!"

"Yes, yes, no school, no school!" erupted the rest of the students.

"There will be no demonstrations in this school," the principal said authoritatively. "We've had enough bloodshed in Soweto already."

"The struggle in Soweto is our struggle too," some students clamored. "The Afrikaans decree applies to us as well. We too want an equal education. The bloody Boers should stop force-feeding us slave education. To hell with Afrikaans! To hell with Afrikaans!" The cry infected everybody. Students began organizing into groups to plot strategy for a peaceful rally in solidarity with our brothers and sisters in Soweto. The principal tried to restore order but was ignored. Most teachers helped us with the planning of the rally. "Be peaceful and orderly," one teacher said, "or else you'll have the whole Boer army down your necks in no time."

We painted placards that condemned Bantu Education, Afrikaans and apartheid. We demanded an equal education with whites. We urged the government to stop the killings in Soweto. Student leaders were chosen to lead the march to other schools in the area, where we planned to pick up more students for a rally at a nearby stadium. Within an hour we had filled the street and formed columns. We began marching.

"*AMANDLA! AWETHU! AMANDLA! AWETHU!*" we chanted and waved placards.

From government buildings nearby white people who headed the Tembisa city councils hurriedly stepped out, jumped into cars and zoomed off under police escort. Our ranks swelled with youths who didn't attend school. Black men and women cheered and exhorted us from yards alongside the streets. "TO HELL WITH A FOURTH-CLASS EDUCATION!" "STOP THE GENOCIDE IN SOWETO!"

"AMANDLA! AWETHU! AMANDLA! AWETHU!" The cries reverberated through the air.

We picked up hundreds of students from other schools and then headed for the stadium. As the river of black faces coursed through the street leading to the stadium, a group of police vans and trucks suddenly appeared from nowhere and barricaded the street.

"Don't panic! Don't panic!" the student leaders yelled at the restless crowd. "Let's remain peaceful and orderly. They'll leave us alone if we don't provoke them."

Policemen with riot gear, rifles, tear gas canisters and *sjamboks* poured out of the trucks and formed a phalanx across the wide street. As in Soweto, most of them were black. From one of the trucks the husky voice of a white man suddenly boomed through a megaphone: "DISPERSE AND RETURN TO YOUR HOMES AND SCHOOLS! OR WE'LL BE FORCED TO USE FORCE!"

A few students started turning back, but the majority stood and waited, chanting defiantly with fists raised in the black power salute. We began singing, *"Nkosi*

Sikelel'i Afrika" ("God Bless Africa"), the ANC's anthem:

> *God bless Africa*
> *Raise up our descendants*
> *Hear our prayers.*
> *Come, holy spirit,*
> *Come, holy spirit,*
> *Lord bless us,*
> *Us, your children.*

The police charged. Several shots rang out. Pandemonium broke out. Students fled for cover. It rained tear gas canisters. David and I managed to flee into one of the nearby yards, jumped its fence and ran all the way to school, where teachers told us to go home immediately, for police were raiding schools. The bus stop was a mile or so away. As we made our way through the matchbox-type Tembisa houses, we saw fires and palls of black smoke in the distance. Some beer halls and vehicles had been gutted.

"I hope there's still a bus out of this place," David panted.

We found what turned out to be one of the last buses out of Tembisa, for the police were quarantining the ghetto, barring all company vehicles and public transportation. On our way to Alexandra there was unusual traffic on the highway leading to the Jan Smuts Airport.

"White folks are fleeing by the droves," I remarked.

"They're afraid this whole thing may turn into a revolution," David replied.

Approaching Alexandra, we saw several armoured cars formed into roadblocks, sealing all the roads leading in and out of Alexandra. All vehicles were being stopped and searched. Our bus was stopped, and several soldiers in camouflage uniforms, carrying automatic weapons, ordered us out and lined us up alongside the body of the bus. I shook like a leaf. In the distance, Alexandra resembled a battlefield. Smoke and fire engulfed the area, and from time to time, the sound of gunfire reverberated through the clouds of smoke.

"You'll have to walk home," one of the white soldiers ordered us. "Buses can't go in there. You bloody Kaffirs are burning down everything."

We immediately headed homeward across the veld. From time to time, people glanced nervously over their shoulders, afraid of being shot in the back. When

David and I entered Alexandra, we saw several burning government buildings, beer halls, schools, stores belonging to Indians and Chinamen. A bus had been overturned and set afire. People were looting all around, making off with drums of paraffin, bags of mealie meal, carcasses of beef still dripping blood, Primus stoves, boxes of canned goods, loaves of bread and so on. There was power and energy in men, women and children that I had never seen before.

The rebellion had begun in Alexandra.

Over the next few days, it spread to black ghettos in other parts of the country: Pretoria, Springs, Daveyton, Kwa-Thema, Durban, Port Elizabeth, Cape Town. Schools, clinics, government buildings, beer halls, stores belonging to whites, Indians and Chinamen, PUTCO buses, Coca-Cola and other delivery trucks—all went up in flames. Black schooling came to a virtual standstill.

Without schooling the student movement was better able to coordinate its activities. Marches were planned, demonstrations were held, and the black work force was urged to stop working in solidarity with student grievances.

"Our struggle is your struggle," exhorted student leaders. "If we unite and work together, we can and will bring down this evil system. We can defeat the whites. Unity is strength."

At first, black workers were supportive of the students and stayed away from jobs. But gradually, due largely to threats of dismissal from jobs, the need for money to survive and intimidation and beatings by the police, many black men and women returned to work.

The police even succeeded in turning some black workers against the students. In Soweto Zulu migrant workers were reported to have formed vigilante groups and, with police license, hacked, stabbed and clubbed students to death. To some extent the same thing happened in Alexandra. As black fought against black, Alexandra was sealed off by armoured vehicles and soldiers, to prevent the violence and carnage from spilling into the suburbs, where whites were buying shotguns and rifles. Many were reported leaving the country every day. Each night Prime Minister Vorster and Minister of Police Kruger went on radio to reassure panic-stricken whites that the situation in the ghettos would soon be brought under control.

The death toll mounted. One hundred . . . one hundred and fifty . . . two hundred killed. The more of us they murdered the more bitter and angry we became, and the more we fought on and the more destruction we wreaked. Black schools were ordered closed indefinitely; that is, those that hadn't yet gone up in flames.

Black informers began to mushroom all over the place. In order to stay alive black people sold each other to the white man. The student movement was infiltrated, its leaders arrested in massive predawn raids and detained without trial. New laws went into effect specifically designed to quell black anger. Journalists and teachers and community leaders were arrested along with students. Without leaders the student movement became disorganized.

Each day I found myself in the company of bloodthirsty mobs. I had lost control of myself and seemed possessed by a sinister force, which made me mindless of my safety, which spurred me toward reckless action, unafraid of death.

We had no guns, *sjamboks*, tear gas or armoured vehicles, but we soon learned how to make petrol bombs. The orgy of violence and destruction and killing continued unabated.

One morning I followed a mob that was going about the ghetto, burning and looting stores and butcher shops belonging to Indians and Chinese, who everyone thought had become rich through cheating and overcharging black peasants. One such Chinese family (the same I had worked for) owned several stores and butcher shops on Twelfth Avenue. The family had fled the first day the riots broke out, and had left three vicious dogs to guard their property behind a high fence. When the mob arrived at the property several out-of-work men and *tsotsis* who were our leaders conferred on what to do with the dogs in order to break into the stores. One of the out-of-work men had apparently worked there after me and he said, "I used to feed and wash these dogs every day. They love meat." A chunk of meat was promptly found and poison spread all over it. It was then thrown over to the dogs, who apparently hadn't eaten anything since their owner fled. They devoured the poisoned meat, much to the jubilation of the crowd. While the dogs groaned and gasped the

fence was cut and the mob poured in.
Several *tsotsis*, armed with machetes,
hacked the dying dogs into bloody pulps.

"I wish the Chinaman was here," one of
them said deliriously.

For an instant I became aware of the
senselessness of what we were doing. But
those misgivings gave way to euphoria as I
saw black peasants making off with plun-
dered goods. I joined in. While the mob
looted furiously, word came that several
army trucks were headed in our direction.
Having found little loot thus far, a couple
friends and I lingered while the rest of the
mob fled.

Moments later we too left, lugging the
spoils of our scavenging. On the way home
we linked up with another group, mostly
girls and women, who had just raided an
Indian shop nearby. Everyone was happy.
Everyone now had precious food to last a
while. Even the destitute could now boast
of owning something. I scanned the faces
around me and saw the poverty of hate and
anger mirrored in them. "These are the
makers of a revolution," I said to myself,
recalling the movie *A Tale of Two Cities*. If it
had not been for the cordon the army had
formed around Alexandra, there would

have been a massacre of whites. I could see the guillotine and tribunals of black peasants.

As we headed home people said to one another:

"This paraffin drum will keep the family going for months."

"This bag of mealie meal will last forever."

"I don't know where I'll store this meat," complained someone who was lugging a whole carcass of a sheep over his shoulder. "We don't even have a bathtub where we could put it in some ice."

"Just go to a store that sells bathtubs and take one," came the reply.

"I have enough candles to light up the whole [of] Alexandra."

"I have enough Coca-Cola to drown myself in."

"My little twin sisters won't have to cry all night because I have enough infant formula to replace my mother's dry breasts."

"The rats will wish they had never invaded our house. This bag of Rotex will wipe them off the surface of the earth."

As the crowd of looters made its way down Twelfth Avenue, a cry suddenly went up: "The army is coming! The army is coming!"

Suddenly shots rang out. Tear gas canisters dropped in our midst like hailstones. People abandoned their loot and ran for cover. Several young girls, including two who lived in my yard, ran confusedly about the street, coughing and choking from all the tear gas.

"Run this way! Run this way!" several people screamed at the girls. I was busy soaking my shirt at a nearby communal tap so as to combat the effects of tear gas. More shots rang out. More tear gas. I ran into a tin-and-plastic shack nearby.

"Why are you doing all this?" mumbled the owner of the shack, a grey-haired old man in a threadbare coat, with deformed legs and a bent back. "You know that the police are out to kill all of you."

"It's hunger and hate and anger, Ntate [Father]," I said, peeping through the grimy window at the teargas-enveloped street.

"They'll kill you all," he repeated. "Yeah, that's what white people want to do, kill us all."

"We'll kill some of them too, Ntate," I said, still peering through the window.

"What is it you children are fighting for,

anyway?" he said, hawking up phlegm and swallowing it.

"To be free, *Ntate*," I said. "We're fighting so that you, me and every black man, woman and child in this country can lead a life of dignity."

"It can never be done," the old man shook his head. "The white man will always rule. The freedom struggle is dead."

"It's been reborn in us, *Ntate*," I said. "We'll pick up the flame of liberation and march onward to victory."

"That can never be done," the old man said. "You should not sacrifice your young lives for something that can never be."

"Freedom *will* come to South Africa, *Ntate*," I vowed. "Azania will be born, and we, the young ones, will do it. To die fighting for one's freedom is no sacrifice, for life without freedom isn't worth living. We've been under the white man's yoke for too long, *Ntate*; it's time we tore the chains."

While talking to the old man, I had taken my eyes off the street. Suddenly I saw something that made me start with horror. I said to the old man, in a trembling voice, "Is there any quick way out of this yard beside through the gate?"

"Yes, why?" the old man said.

"I just saw a girl I know being dragged away by the police," I said. "And I think she's dead, but I'm not sure. There was blood all over her dress."

The old man's mouth dropped in horror. "Oh, God! Oh, God!" he cried. "What's the world coming to? What are they doing to us?"

"How do I get out?" I insisted. "I've got to get to her home and tell her parents."

The old man told me there was a small opening in the fence near the lavatories in the back of the yard, which led to Eleventh Avenue; and from there, if I was extremely careful, I could make my way to Thirteenth Avenue in no time.

I reached Mashudu's home only to find her family moaning. Apparently the tragic news had already reached them—the twelve-year-old schoolgirl was indeed dead.

The next day her parents went to the police station to claim the body for burial and were told to pay for it.

She was buried that Sunday, under cloudy skies and an intermittent drizzle. Even though police had banned all gatherings of more than three people, including

those of families who wanted to bury their
loved ones, hundreds attended Mashudu's
funeral, mostly her schoolmates. We carried the small brown coffin shoulder high,
intoning African liberation songs. As it was
being lowered into the six-foot grave, the
preacher, a grey-haired old man with fire
in his eyes, said the following eulogy:

"In her, as in hundreds of other black
children who have died since this whole
nightmare began, had been embodied the
hope for a better Africa. Give us strength
and courage, O Lord, to triumph over our
enemies, our oppressors. Let this child's
death, and all the others, be not in vain. Let
there come out of all this spilled innocent
blood a new South Africa, where we can
live in dignity and freedom. As you receive
her soul into your bosom, O mighty God,
send us the weapons to carry on the struggle against injustice, to carry on till all
Africans are liberated. Out of dust we
came, back to dust we return. . . ."

As the grave was sealed, it occurred to
me that it could easily have been me or any
of my siblings in it. I shook with rage and
hatred. Why did they kill her, why? I asked
myself. She was so young, so full of life and
promise. I used to play with her when I was

growing up; I had called her "my wife" many times when we played house with other children in the yard. Now she was gone, her life snuffed by a white man's bullet.

Tears streamed down my face. I wondered what direction my life would take now. As the crowd sang *"Nkosi Sikelel'i Afrika,"* I heard Mashudu's brother vow, "They'll pay for this." After the funeral I went back home, shut myself in the bedroom and questioned a belief I had long cherished: that there was a place in South Africa for the teachings of Mahatma Gandhi, that what Martin Luther King, Jr., had done for blacks in America could be done for blacks in South Africa.

No, I was all wrong. The black man's freedom from apartheid could be attained only through the barrel of a gun, amid rivers of blood. The doctrine of nonviolence, of passive resistance, couldn't work against the Boers. To be free, we had to fight the white man, shed his blood, vanquish him on the battlefield. Do I have the courage to kill another human being? I asked myself. My mind refused to answer the question.

Glossary

Afrikaans. (Af-ri-KANS) The language of white South Africans of Dutch descent. It is similar to the present-day Dutch language.

ANC. Stands for the African National Congress. The ANC seeks to abolish apartheid and to create a true democracy for South Africans of all races. In 1960, the ANC was outlawed. In 1990, it was made legal. Nelson Mandela is the Deputy President of the organization.

apartheid. (a-PAR-tate) The system in South Africa that the white government set up to insure white domination of the country. It requires total separation of the races.

Azania. (A-ZANE-ee-uh) A name for South Africa. It first appeared hundreds of years ago when the first maps of the area were drawn. Some of the groups fighting for South African freedom want to change the name of the country to Azania.

Bantu. (BAN-too) A group of native Africans and the language they speak.

Boer. (BO-uhr) A white South African of Dutch descent. *Boer* is the Dutch word for *farmer.*

Coloureds. A degrading term used for mixed-race people.

genocide. (JEN-uh-side) The deliberate destruction of a people because of their race, culture or beliefs.

Kaffir. (KAF-er) A degrading term used by many South African whites to refer to blacks. ("I was called a 'Kaffir' many times," Mark Mathabane wrote. "It is equivalent to the term nigger.")

Khoikhoi. (KOY-koy) A tribal group.

mealie meal. Corn meal.

Msomi. (Muh-SO-mee) Black gangsters who operated like the Mafia.

Ntate. (in-TAH-tay) "Father" in the Sotho language.

paraffin. (PAR-uh-fin) Kerosene. Used as a fuel for lamps and for stoves.

petrol. (PET-roll) Gasoline.

Primus. (PRY-mus) A kind of stove that burns kerosene.

PUTCO. Stands for the Public Utility Transportation Company that operates bus lines.

sjambok. (SHAM-bok) An animal-hide whip.

tsotsis. (TSO-tsees) Hoodlums. People who treat others roughly or brutally.

veld. A grassy field.

vigilante. (vij-uh-LAN-tee) A person who is not a law officer who takes the law into his or her own hands.

Zulu. (ZOO-loo) A group of native Africans and the Bantu language they speak.

Questions for the Reader

THINKING ABOUT THE STORY

1. What was interesting for you about the selections from *Kaffir Boy*?

2. Were there ways the events or people in the selections became important or special to you? Write about or discuss these.

3. What do you think were the most important things Mark Mathabane wanted to say in the selections?

4. In what ways did the selections answer the questions you had before you began reading or listening?

5. Were any parts of the selections difficult to understand? If so, you may want to read or listen to them again. Discuss with your learning partners possible reasons why they were difficult.

THINKING ABOUT THE WRITING

1. How did Mark Mathabane help you see, hear and feel what happened in the selections? Find the words, phrases or sentences that did this best.

2. Writers think carefully about their stories' settings, characters and events. In writing these selections, which of these things do you think Mark Mathabane felt was most important? Find the parts of the story that support your opinion.

3. In the selections, Mark Mathabane uses dialogue. Dialogue can make a story stronger and more alive. Pick out some dialogue that you feel is strong, and explain how it helps the story.

4. Mark Mathabane, through his writing, makes us feel his fear and excitement at different ages. Find some parts in the selections that helped you feel this fear or excitement.

ACTIVITIES

1. Were there any words that were diffi-
    cult for you in the selections from
    Kaffir Boy? Go back to these words
    and try to figure out their meanings.
    Discuss what you think each word
    means, and why you made that guess.
    Look them up in a dictionary and see
    if your definitions are the same or
    different.

    Discuss with your learning partners
    how you are going to remember each
    word. Some ways to remember words
    are to put them on file cards, write
    them in a journal, or create a person-
    al dictionary. Be sure to use the
    words in your writing in a way that
    will help you to remember their
    meaning.

2. Talking with other people about what
    you have read can increase your un-
    derstanding. Discussion can help you
    organize your thoughts, get new ideas
    and rethink your original ideas. Dis-
    cuss your thoughts about the selec-
    tions with someone else who has
    read them. Find out if you helped

yourself understand the selections in the same or different ways. Find out if your opinions about the selections are the same or different. See if your thoughts change as a result of this discussion.

3. After you finish reading or listening, you might want to write down your thoughts about the book. You could write your reflections on the book in a journal, or you could write about topics the book has brought up that you want to explore further. You could write a book review or a letter to a friend you think might be interested in the book.

4. Did reading the selections give you any ideas for your own writing? You might want to write about:

- the way it would feel to be white or black in South Africa.
- an exciting or frightening event from your childhood.
- a decision you made to help yourself or other people overcome injustice.

5. You might want to read a newspaper or magazine article on events in

South Africa or another African country. You might think about the ways an article about an event is different from reading an eyewitness account of it. List these differences in a journal and discuss them with others.

6. If you could talk to Mark Mathabane, what questions would you ask about his writing? You might want to write the questions in a journal.

About Mark Mathabane

In June 1990, 30-year-old Mark Mathabane was interviewed on a radio talk show in New York. The talk show host asked him how he had been able to pull himself out of the terrible poverty of the Alexandra ghetto. Mathabane said that it was the result of his parents' refusal to let his family be broken up by the laws of apartheid. He also said that his mother helped by teaching him the lessons of survival:

> self-reliance (learning to take care of himself)
> self-motivation (doing things to help himself)
> belief in himself
> discipline
> responsibility.

In *Kaffir Boy*, Mathabane tells of many situations in which he became discouraged. Each time, his mother would urge him to overcome his fears and go on to better himself. She taught him the lessons of survival all through his life.

An important change in his life came when Mark Mathabane was 14. He had a job doing housework in a white family's home. One day Mrs. Smith, the white woman who employed him, gave him a tennis racquet she no longer used. He found that he enjoyed hitting balls against a wall and worked hard to become skillful at tennis.

Several people, black and white, noticed that Mathabane was becoming a good player. They helped him by giving him equipment and lessons, and by allowing him to play in some of the white tennis clubs.

Then, Mathabane met Stan Smith, an American tennis star and former Wimbledon champion. Smith and his wife, Marjory, were impressed not only by Mathabane's tennis skill but also by his intelligence and personality.

The Smiths were soon to return to the United States and told Mark that they would try to get him a tennis scholarship there.

Finally, with the help of the Smiths and other Americans, Mathabane received a scholarship to Limestone College in South Carolina. On September 16, 1978, at the age of 18, he boarded an airplane to America.

About leaving South Africa, Mathabane says in *Kaffir Boy:* "After eighteen years of living life as a fourth-class citizen, a slave in the land of apartheid, I was at last leaving for another world, a different way of life, a better existence, away from bondage."

From Limestone College, Mathabane later transferred to Quincy College in Illinois, and then to Dowling College on Long Island, New York. At Dowling, he became the first black editor of the student newspaper.

By the time he graduated, he had become a skilled writer. He wrote about something he knew well: growing up black in South Africa. The stories he wrote became the book *Kaffir Boy,* which was published in 1986. After Mark Mathabane's television appearance on *The Oprah Winfrey Show,* the book became a bestseller.

In 1987, he married an American writer, Gail Ernsberger, whom he had met in New York. He continues writing and lecturing. His latest book, *African Women: Three Generations,* was published in 1994.

About South Africa

South Africa is a country that covers the southern end of the continent of Africa. It has a population of 44.5 million, of whom 5.8 million are white, and 38.7 million are people of color.

South Africa today is one of the richest countries in the world. But for most of its people—its people of color—it is one of the poorest.

People have lived in southern Africa for thousands of years. There were many different groups of people, each with its own language and culture. They made their living by farming and hunting and they controlled their own land and lives.

Around 350 years ago, all this began to change. In 1652, Dutch people from Holland established a colony on the land at the tip of southern Africa. It was called the Cape Colony. In those days, trading ships from the Dutch East India Company sailed around the tip of Africa on their way to and from their colonies in Asia. The Cape Colony was established because these ships needed a place to get fresh water and food for the long journey.

The African peoples who lived on the cape in those days were the Khoikhoi and the San. The Khoikhoi raised cattle and the San hunted for a living.

Labor was very scarce in the Cape Colony. In order to get the workers they needed, the Dutch imported slaves from other parts of Africa and from Asian countries. By the time slavery was abolished in South Africa in 1807, more than 35,000 people had been held in bondage. To control these slaves, the Dutch made the first laws in southern Africa requiring black people to carry passes to travel between the towns and the countryside.

As the Cape Colony grew, the Dutch took over more and more of the land used by the Khoikhoi and the San. The Dutch turned the land into large farms. The Africans fought back, but they were eventually defeated.

The Dutch settlers were soon joined by other European settlers from Great Britain. The British, like the Dutch, had colonies in Asia. They wanted to control southern Africa to protect the route of their ships to Asia. In 1795, British troops arrived in the Cape Colony and the British finally took it over in 1814.

As more whites settled in southern Africa, there was less farmland available in the Cape Colony. Around 1836 many white farmers, descendants of the Dutch settlers called Boers, moved out of the Cape Colony. They went north and east farther into southern Africa to get more land. This brought them into conflict with other African peoples—among them the Xhosa, Zulu and Sotho.

In cruel, bloody wars that went on over many years, the Boers took over more and more land where native Africans had lived for centuries. This land was turned into enormous plantations and farms. The once self-sufficient Africans could no longer make a living from raising crops or herding livestock on their own land.

Around 1870 another great development changed the ways the southern African peoples lived. It was the discovery of diamonds and gold. Workers were needed to dig this wealth out of the earth. Thousands of men were recruited from the poor parts of southern Africa and from neighboring countries to work in the mines owned by the British. By 1895, 100,000 Africans were working in the mines.

As the Dutch and British took over the land and wealth of southern Africa, special laws were passed that controlled where Africans could live and work. These laws kept Africans from settling down in places where they could build secure homes and communities. See the chapter "About Apartheid" on page 60 for more information about this.

During these years, four different governments had come to control four different parts of southern Africa. Two of the governments were run by the British and two by the Boers. The British wanted all four to be united into one republic, but the Boers did not.

The Boers wanted to remain independent. They had developed their own culture and language. They called themselves Afrikaners.

In October 1899, the British and the Boers went to war. The war lasted until 1902 when the Boers finally signed a peace treaty and a unification of the four governments was begun. This was the start of the Republic of South Africa that we know today.

This new government represented the Afrikaners and British, but not the Africans. They remained poor, without land and without rights, denied citizenship in the land of their ancestors.

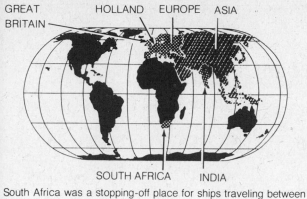

South Africa was a stopping-off place for ships traveling between Europe and Asia.

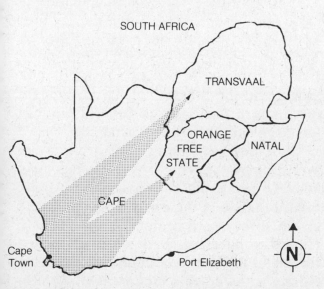

In 1837, the Boers moved north and west into the territory of the Zulu, Xhosa and Soto.

About Apartheid

Apartheid means "separateness" in Afrikaans, the language of the Afrikaners. This word was first used in 1947 to describe the South African government policy of the separation of two groups of people: whites and blacks.

In South Africa, the white population is made up of the Afrikaners and the English. The blacks include all people of color. These are: all the different African peoples; the Coloureds, who are a mixed-race group; and the Indians, who were brought to southern Africa from India as indentured servants beginning around 1860.

From the viewpoint of most of the white population, apartheid was necessary. Whites were a minority in southern Africa. From the time of the first European settlers in the seventeenth century to the present, forced separation had made it easier for whites to control the country. Population figures showed this clearly: Only about 14% of the South African population was white, but this minority controlled the government. Black people were not allowed to vote on the laws that affected their lives.

In 1948, laws were passed that required total separation of the races. Blacks have had to live in designated areas of cities and the countryside—usually the least desirable parts. They have had separate schools, restaurants, buses, toilets and other public facilities. And they have had to carry passbooks so that the police and other government agencies could keep track of them.

Another aspect of apartheid has to do with "homelands." These are areas in remote parts of the country, each set aside for specific tribal groups. The government forced more and more Africans to move to these areas. By 1988 approximately 14 million Africans lived in the homelands.

There are few opportunities for people to make a living in the homelands.

Over the years, many organizations have struggled against the apartheid system. One of these groups is the African National Congress (ANC).

In 1960, the government outlawed antiapartheid groups including the ANC. Thousands of opponents of apartheid were jailed and many of them were tortured in prison. Nelson Mandela, a leader of the ANC, and other anti-apartheid leaders who escaped arrest were forced to work in secret. In 1962, Mandela himself was arrested and later sentenced to prison for life.

Despite the jailing of many of its leaders, the anti-apartheid struggle did not end. In 1976, black students organized huge protests that won worldwide attention and support. Since then, blacks have become even more united in working for their rights. Black organizations, including trade unions, have carried out massive demonstrations and strikes against the government.

With the growth of the anti-apartheid movement within South Africa, more and more people all over the world opposed the apartheid system. Many governments have applied pressure on the South African government by boycotting South African products and by forbidding their companies and banks from doing business with South Africa.

In September 1989, F. W. de Klerk was elected president of the Republic of South Africa. De Klerk convinced the government to start repealing some of its most repressive apartheid laws.

In 1990, as the result of strong pressure from inside and outside South Africa, De Klerk released Mandela and other anti-apartheid leaders from prison. The government also dropped the laws that outlawed political groups such as the ANC.

In 1994, elections were held. People of all races voted. Nelson Mandela was elected as South Africa's first black president.